WHAT THE FUTURE HOLDS

THE FUTURE OF TRANSPORTATION:

FROM ELECTRIC CARS TO JET PACKS

BY ALICIA Z. KLEPEIS
CONTENT CONSULTANT:
PETER C. BISHOP, PH.D., APF
TEACHTHEFUTURE.ORG
HOUSTONFUTURES.ORG

CAPSTONE PRESS
a capstone imprint

Capstone Captivate is published by Capstone Press, an imprint of Capstone.
1710 Roe Crest Drive, North Mankato, Minnesota 56003
www.capstonepub.com

Copyright © 2020 by Capstone. All rights reserved. No part of this publication may be reproduced in whole or in part, or stored in a retrieval system, or transmitted in any form or by any means, electronic, mechanical, photocopying, recording, or otherwise, without written permission of the publisher.

Library of Congress Cataloging-in-Publication Data is available on the Library of Congress website.
ISBN 978-1-5435-9222-1 (library binding)
ISBN 978-1-4966-6626-0 (paperback)
ISBN 978-1-5435-9226-9 (eBook PDF)

Summary: Describes what the future may hold in the area of transportation, including technological advancements and human impact.

Image Credits
Alamy: chombosan, 39, Imaginechina Limited, 23, 29, Naeblys, 7; iStockphoto: AmandaLewis, 5; Newscom: akg-images, 17 (bottom), Cover Images/Aerion, 27 (top), dpa/picture-alliance, 15 (bottom), MEGA/Orion Span, 41, Reuters/Stephen Hird, 31, Reuters/Stephen Lam, 9, WENN.com/ZSB, 17 (top), ZUMA Press/Ferrari, 27 (bottom), ZUMA Press/Robin Utrecht, 19; Science Source: Henning Dalhoff, 43 (top); Shutterstock: andrey_l, 25, Chesky, 35, cyo bo, 21, EQRoy, 33, Everett Historical, 15 (top), metamorworks, Cover, photonewman, 43 (bottom), StockStudio, 13, View Apart, 11; Wikimedia: ToSch1983 Deutsches Zentrum für Luft- und Raumfahrt, 37

Design Elements
Shutterstock: nanmulti, Zeynur Babayev

Editorial Credits
Editor: Mandy Robbins; Designer: Kay Fraser; Media Researcher: Jo Miller; Production Specialist: Laura Manthe

All internet sites appearing in back matter were available and accurate when this book was sent to press.

Printed in the United States of America.
PA100

TABLE OF CONTENTS

INTRODUCTION
CHANGES IN TRANSPORTATION 4

CHAPTER 1
WHAT IS JUST AHEAD? 8

CHAPTER 2
WHAT DOES THE FUTURE HOLD? 20

CHAPTER 3
WHAT IS WAY OUT THERE? 34

TIMELINE 44
GLOSSARY 46
READ MORE 47
INTERNET SITES 47
INDEX 48

Words in bold are in the glossary.

INTRODUCTION
CHANGES IN TRANSPORTATION

How might transportation look in the years to come? People have made many bold predictions. Some were not quite right. In 1958, *Popular Science* magazine predicted people might soon be able to fly using jet packs. But human-powered individual flight has never become reliable or popular. Jet packs have remained loud, heavy, and very expensive.

Other predictions have been closer to the truth. In the 1930s, some people said self-driving cars would be in use by the 1960s. The timeline was wrong, but fully self-driving cars do exist today. They're not legal to use on public streets, though. Another prediction came from the 1962 television cartoon *The Jetsons*. The show was set in 2062. Characters moved from one room to another inside vacuum tubes. This is similar to an up-and-coming mode of transportation called Hyperloop.

Many exciting advances in transportation technology may lie just ahead. From flying taxis to high-speed trains, change could happen fast.

A young man demonstrates a Gravity Industries jet pack in Basingstoke, UK, in 2019.

FUTURES STUDIES

Historians study the past. Futurists study the future. How can you study what hasn't happened yet? Futurists analyze what is happening today. They think about issues that might come up in the future. Using social science and imagination, they create different scenarios, or stories, of what the future could be like.

Some futurists have ideas of what the future of transportation could look like. They look at all aspects of **transit**. They try to figure out how to get people more quickly from place to place. For example, what kinds of transit could avoid traffic? Futurists also look at safer modes of transportation. They study nonpolluting methods of transportation and look at what technology is currently being developed. Futures studies is a growing field. In the coming years, futurists may help travelers find the most efficient ways to move around the world.

In the future, people may travel in Hyperloop capsules. With this system, capsules would move at high speeds inside special tubes.

CHAPTER 1
WHAT IS JUST AHEAD?

SELF-DRIVING CARS

Self-driving cars will likely be important in future transportation. This idea isn't new. The 1939 World's Fair featured an exhibit on self-driving technology. It showed **autonomous** driving in cities of the future.

Most people haven't used totally self-driving cars. But some self-driving features are common in today's vehicles. Adaptive cruise control can adjust a car's speed based on the speed of the cars in front of it. The automatic parking feature tells a driver if a parking space is big enough for the car. It may also automatically steer the car into that spot.

In the future, cars may become fully autonomous. Google has tested its self-driving cars on public roads in several states, including Arizona, Nevada, and California since 2012. Other companies, such as Uber, are testing self-driving cars too.

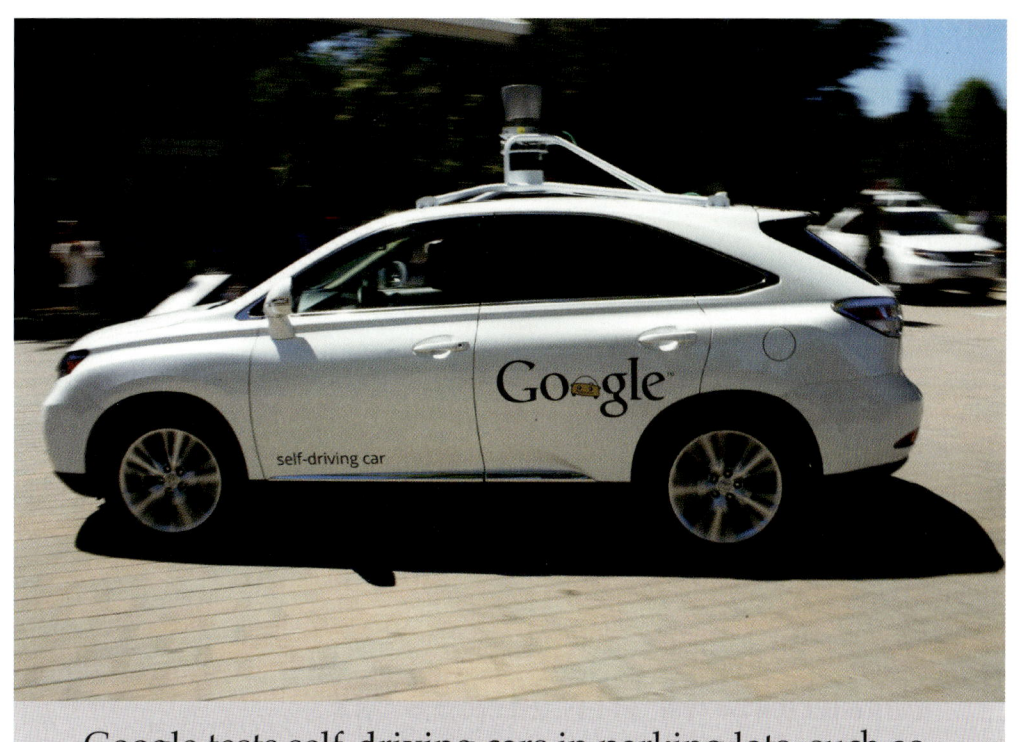

Google tests self-driving cars in parking lots, such as this one in Mountain View, California.

HOW SELF-DRIVING CARS WORK

Human drivers use their brains to operate cars. But self-driving cars have computer "brains." These computers process information from many sources, including cameras, lasers, radar, and more. Most self-driving cars send out laser beams in all directions. Doing this lets the car map out what's around it. Then the car can tell whether a car, a bicycle, a building, or another object is nearby. This information helps a car's computer figure out when to speed up, brake, and change lanes.

THE NEED FOR BETTER TECH

The technology exists for self-driving cars. So why aren't more people using them? The tech hasn't been perfected quite yet. Experts think early models of self-driving cars will work well on freeways. But navigating in cities is more complicated. Self-driving cars would have to deal with more unexpected events. Designers will need to make improvements so these cars work better in urban settings.

ADVANTAGES TO SELF-DRIVING CARS

There are many advantages to driverless cars. One is time. People traveling in self-driving cars can get work done. They can read or even nap. Self-driving cars could also help improve the flow of traffic. They could communicate with other vehicles and traffic lights. This would help them choose routes with less traffic. Self-driving cars could also save lives. More than 90 percent of traffic deaths are due to human error.

Self-driving cars would have many more obstacles to navigate around on busy city streets than on long stretches of open road.

FACT
According to some sources, nine out of 10 car crashes could be eliminated by driverless technology.

MOVING CARGO WITH AUTONOMOUS SHIPS

Most people don't travel by sea regularly. But ships carry more than 90 percent of the world's traded goods. Today's ships have captains and crew members on board. But many people believe that cargo ships could one day run themselves. Computers could control the ships of the future instead of people.

Automation has many advantages. Companies could save money by not having to pay crew members. Unmanned vessels could also be lighter. This could reduce fuel costs. But there are challenges to autonomous shipping. What if an accident happens? There would be no one on site to help out. An autonomous ship may have to change its route quickly because of a storm. The ship's control systems might be taken over by pirates. Engineers must find ways to address all of these possibilities before ships can sail themselves.

The *Luna Maersk* cargo ship transports goods across the Mediterranean Sea.

THE YARA BIRKELAND

A large electric ship called the *Yara Birkeland* was under construction in 2019. It is set to carry fertilizer between cities in Norway. It can hold 120 shipping containers. The *Yara Birkeland* is due to be completed in 2020. It will have a crew at first. But the goal is for the ship to be fully autonomous by 2022.

CARGO AIRSHIPS

In 1852, the first **airship** took flight. This steam-powered flying machine was 143 feet (44 meters) long. Airships carried people and cargo. During World War I (1914–1918), airships used hydrogen to stay afloat. Hydrogen is highly flammable. Several disasters led to airships losing popularity, including the explosion of the Hindenburg in 1937.

Airships have changed a lot since their early days. Back then, they were not very practical, so they weren't used often. Now airships use helium to provide lift, which is much safer. Today's airships need few if any crew members. They can take off and land nearly anywhere. New airships could move huge cargo loads by the early 2020s. They could deliver all of the wood beams needed to build a house or a farmer's entire harvest of fruits or vegetables.

FACT
The up-and-coming Flying Whales airship is twice the length of a Boeing 747 jumbo jet. It can hold cargo inside or sling it below the airship.

The Hindenburg went up in flames on May 6, 1937. This disaster killed 35 people.

Airships such as the Skyship 600 are currently used for advertising.

FLYING CARS

In 1964, science-fiction writer Isaac Asimov predicted that flying cars would be in use by 2014. Widespread use of flying cars is still probably many years away. But **prototypes** of such vehicles are already underway.

Imagine this—a person wants to take a short flight to a destination. Then he wants to finish the journey on local roads. The AeroMobil would allow him to do just that. It can cruise along on roads. It can convert from a car to a plane in three minutes. The AeroMobil can reach 99 miles (160 kilometers) per hour on roads. It reaches 224 miles (360 km) per hour in the air.

People who want to operate flying cars need training. Users often need a driver's license and a pilot's license. This is true for the AeroMobil and the Pal-V Liberty flying cars. Both models will need runways or grass airstrips for takeoff and landing. Several other companies plan to offer flying cars to customers in the next few years. The minimum cost is about $400,000.

The Terrafugia Transition is another vehicle that can fly through the sky and travel on the road.

Henry Ford

HENRY FORD'S FLYING CAR

Henry Ford was a transportation legend. His Model T cars were a big success. But did you know Ford had an idea for a flying car? In 1926, Ford revealed plans for the Ford Flivver. This was supposed to be a flying car for the average person. On February 25, 1928, test pilot Harry J. Brooks was flying the Flivver when it crashed. Brooks died in the crash. Ford never created a successful flying car.

VTOLS AND FLYING TAXIS

Have you ever heard of a VTOL vehicle? *VTOL* stands for "vertical take-off and landing." Flying cars need airstrips to take off and land. But VTOL aircraft can travel straight up from the ground into the sky. Companies are developing different models of VTOL aircraft. None are available to buy yet.

The Pop.Up Next is one VTOL prototype. Airbus is another company that has several prototypes. These vehicles combine self-driving features with the capability of a passenger **drone**. This type of system could be launched within the next 10 years.

Having vehicles that fly and drive could reduce traffic jams on city streets. VTOL vehicles might work great as flying taxis in big cities. Customers could book autonomous flying taxis. Uber plans to start using flying taxis by the mid-2020s.

Government agencies are working on rules and regulations for VTOL vehicles. They want to ensure this new form of transportation would help people travel safely.

Airbus displayed its latest VTOL drone design for public transportation during Amsterdam Drone Week in 2018.

FACT
On average, people in the United States spend more than 40 hours a year stuck in traffic.

CHAPTER 2
WHAT DOES THE FUTURE HOLD?

THE MAGIC OF MAGLEV

Over the next 30 years, transportation will probably become more high tech. More use of **maglev** trains is just one way this could happen.

Imagine traveling aboard a train at more than 175 miles (282 km) per hour. This train has no wheels and no engine. It's quiet and clean. Does this sound like a fantasy? It's not. It's a maglev train. These trains use magnetic levitation to work.

Maglev trains will likely help future travelers reach their destinations fast. How do they work? Magnets are put on the train and along the path where the train will travel. The magnets push the train upward. This creates a gap between the train and the ground. Since the train is not on a track, its wheels don't rub against the rail. That allows for faster speeds.

The United Kingdom was the first country to use a maglev system. It opened one in 1984 to service the Birmingham airport. Maglev trains now run in Japan, China, and South Korea.

Workers in Japan are currently building a maglev line that will run from Tokyo to Osaka. This project could be done by 2045. The 255-mile (410-km) trip would take 1 hour and 7 minutes. That's less than half the time it took to travel that distance by train in 2019!

The Shanghai Maglev in Shanghai, China, has a top operating speed of 268 miles (431 km) per hour.

SUPER MAGLEV: WILL IT HAPPEN?

In the next 50 years, some experts think maglev trains will be common in most major cities. But engineers are trying to build even faster trains. Researchers in China are working on what they call "Super Maglev." Scientists think this line would move a train at speeds of up to 600 miles (966 km) per hour. That would be more than twice the speed of current maglev trains. At this speed, someone could travel between Washington, D.C., and New York City in 20 minutes!

How could super maglevs be so much faster? These trains would run in a vacuum-sealed tube. Traveling in such a tube avoids wind resistance. Super maglevs are in the early stages of testing using a small track. Only time will tell if these superfast trains will be used in the future.

FACT
The China Aerospace Science and Industry Corporation is working on a transit system that could reach speeds of 2,485 miles (4,000 km) per hour.

Professor Deng Zigang (center) poses with his students and the super maglev vehicle they are developing at Southwest Jiaotong University in China.

HYPERLOOP

Waiting to travel on a super maglev train? The Hyperloop will probably be used sooner. These transit systems are similar in many ways. Both will transport passengers at high speeds inside low-pressure tubes. Hyperloop passengers will ride in capsules rather than train-like vehicles. The 98-foot- (30-m-) long capsules can carry 28 to 40 passengers. People have compared the ride to being in a very comfy airplane.

Both systems use magnets to keep the vehicles elevated above the track. Special vacuums in the Hyperloop system remove air inside the tube. This creates a low-pressure environment. Without any air pressing against them, the capsules can move fast and smoothly.

Futurist Ian Pearson expects Hyperloop systems to be common within 30 years. But people won't have to wait that long to try out Hyperloop. As of 2017, five countries were developing Hyperloop routes. The first Hyperloop system is scheduled to launch in 2020 in the United Arab Emirates. This 6-mile (10-km) track will eventually connect to Saudi Arabia.

Because it travels in a tube, the weather would not affect a Hyperloop capsule.

FACT
A proposed Hyperloop route could reduce travel time from Kansas City to St. Louis to just 30 minutes. By car, this trip takes about 3 hours and 40 minutes.

AIRPLANES OF THE FUTURE

Commercial jetliners have looked about the same for more than 50 years. Engines are often below the wings in the middle of the plane. But airplane design is changing. Some changes will make the passengers' experiences better. Like a few current planes, developmental planes such as Aurora's D8 have engines in the back. This makes flights quieter. Planes could also get quicker. Some experts say that without windows, planes of the future would be better able to handle faster speeds.

Rising fuel costs are another reason the look of planes will likely change. Some new airplane designs will be more energy-efficient. For example, a tail-less plane would have less **drag**. It would use less energy. Manufacturers are experimenting with different wing designs too. A blended wing design has a flatter shape than commercial planes today. These planes would likely need less fuel than current models.

> **FACT**
> Some future planes may have massage seats and scents such as fresh pine or sea breeze. Special audio systems could act like noise machines to help people sleep.

Together Boeing and Aerion are creating the AS2. This business jet will fly almost twice as fast as modern passenger planes.

Boom is a company working to build aircraft that fly at superfast speeds. The XB-1 is one of its latest designs.

THE FUTURE OF AVIATION

The future of flight involves more than plane design. **Fossil fuels** power nearly all of today's aircraft. In the next 20 years, electricity might power most aircraft used for short distances. Electric planes will be less expensive to operate than today's aircraft.

There could even be totally pilotless airliners. This could happen in the next 50 years or less. Developing such a plane has many challenges. One is teaching a computer how to deal with the many factors that can arise during a flight. These could include changes in weather or mechanical problems. Another option would be to have someone on the ground controlling the plane with a remote control.

To be financially successful, companies will need to be sure passengers aren't afraid to buy tickets on pilotless planes. One way to combat this fear is to educate people on how little flying pilots actually do now. A recent survey of Boeing and Airbus pilots found that they manually fly for only about 3 to 6 minutes each flight. The plane is flown by a computer in autopilot mode for the rest of the flight.

While there are no electric airliners yet, there are small electric aircraft, such as the Ruixiang RX1E.

FACT
In the next 20 years, at least 600,000 new pilots will be needed to meet the demand for air travel. Pilotless planes could change that figure.

FASTER FLIGHTS

Throughout history, travelers have been trying to get to their destinations faster. Airplane speeds are bound to improve greatly in the next 20 years. In 2017, a passenger jet had an average cruising speed of about 575 miles (925 km) per hour. Future airplanes may fly at **supersonic** speed. That's faster than the speed of sound! This is around 768 miles (1,236 km) per hour.

From 1976 to 2003, an airplane called the Concorde flew at supersonic speed. Its passengers could go from New York City to London in less than 3.5 hours. The Concorde was retired because of how expensive it was to operate and maintain.

Several companies are working to create supersonic aircraft that can fly more cheaply. One example is a Japanese concept aircraft called HYTEX. It could travel five times faster than the speed of sound. One challenge of creating new supersonic aircraft is reducing the noise they make. Another challenge involves heat. Aircraft traveling so fast must be able to withstand extreme surface temperatures.

The Concorde landed its last flight at London's Heathrow Airport on October 24, 2003.

CLEAN & GREEN TRANSPORT

Creating vehicles that pollute less is an important goal for the future. Electric aircraft release fewer greenhouse gas **emissions**. But no electric airliners exist yet. Governments have been making rules that require vehicles to produce fewer emissions. The Norwegian government set a big goal for itself in 2018. It aimed for all flights within Norway to be electric by 2040. More than 100 projects to create electric-powered aircraft are now underway around the world.

Fewer cars will run on fossil fuels in the future. The government of the United Kingdom made a bold announcement in 2017. It said new vehicles that run on fossil fuels would be banned from sale by 2040. Electric-powered cars will likely grow in use. Hydrogen can be used as fuel too. Future cars may also run on **biofuels**. Biofuels can be made from various products. These include corn and sugarcane. They also include animal fats and vegetable oils.

As electric vehicles become more common, so will electric charging stations.

FACT
About 392 million gallons (1.48 billion liters) of gasoline are used each day in the United States.

CHAPTER 3
WHAT IS WAY OUT THERE?

ROADS WITH ADVANCED TECHNOLOGY

Today people often use technology to find routes with the least traffic. Travel **apps** and **Global Positioning System** (GPS) devices do this job well. Road signs help drivers make decisions. Some tell them to slow down or stop. Others note that a detour is ahead. Traffic lights and signs may not be necessary forever. Self-driving cars might not need them to navigate through urban areas.

Imagine a scene in the distant future: A self-driving car approaches an intersection. The car's wireless technology communicates with an "intersection manager." This manager is not a person. It's a computer. As the car approaches the intersection, the computer could read its travel plan. Then the computer would calculate the best route. The vehicle would automatically take this route. This system would save the driver time. It could also keep traffic moving smoothly.

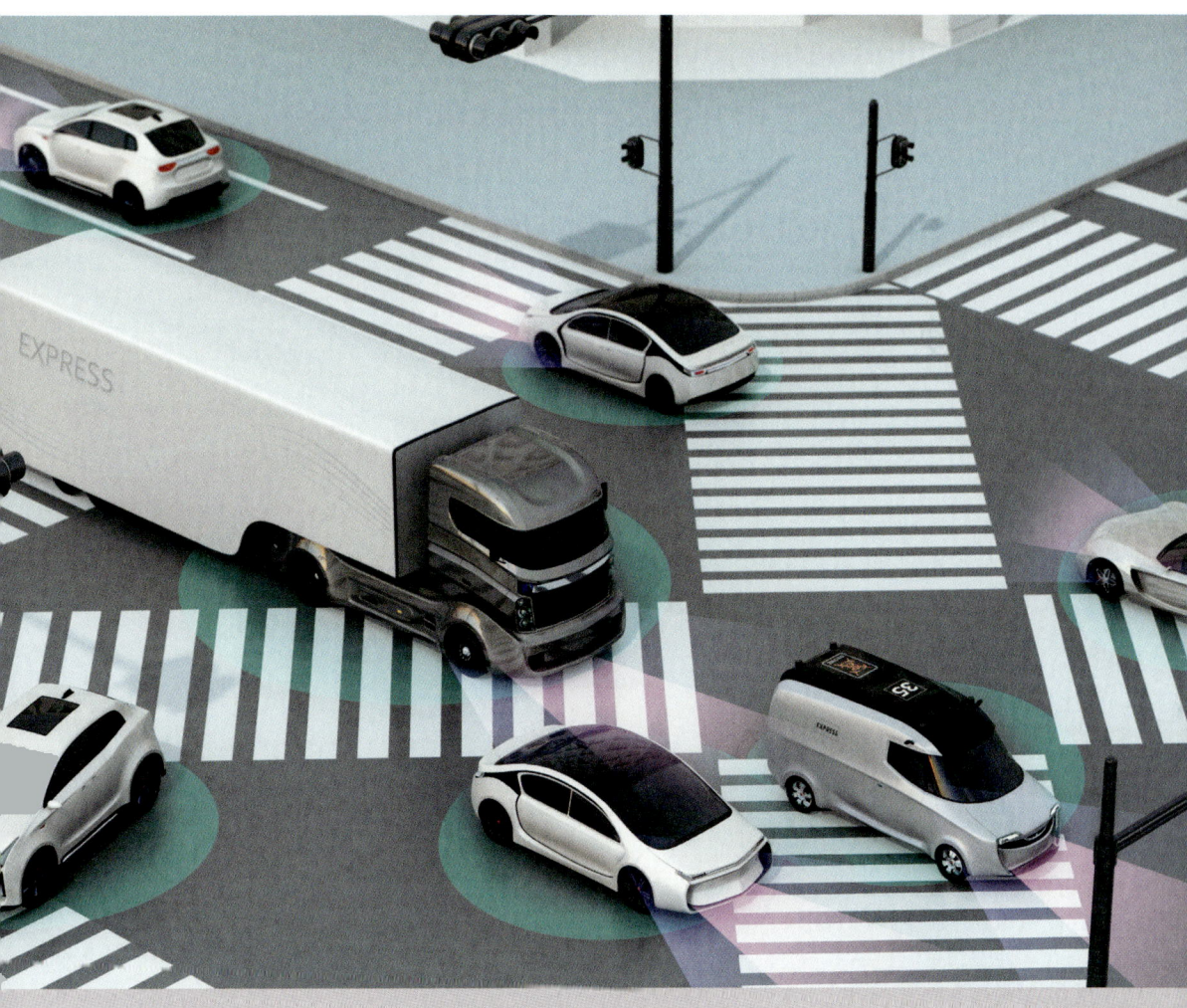
Intersection managers could eliminate the need for any road signs.

SPACELINER

Rocket travel may replace long plane flights many years into the future. The German Aerospace Center is working on a craft called the SpaceLiner. This craft would hold 50 passengers. It would fly unbelievably fast. The SpaceLiner might be able to travel 25 times faster than the speed of sound. At that speed, a person could fly from Australia to London in just 90 minutes!

Eleven rocket engines would propel SpaceLiner during launch. This **booster** stage is when the spacecraft fires its rockets to gain speed. When the booster stage is complete, the passenger vehicle would separate from the nine rocket engines that launched it. SpaceLiner could fly as high as 50 miles (80 km) above Earth's surface. After reaching this height, the passenger part of the vehicle would start coasting down toward its destination.

SpaceLiner aims to be fully operational by 2050. It would be a clean vehicle. This craft would produce no greenhouse gas emissions—only water vapor and hydrogen.

SpaceLiner's design would need to be very sleek in order to reach maximum speed.

FACT
The estimated cost to get the SpaceLiner to the prototype stage is $30 to $32 billion.

COMMUTING AND CHANGES IN CITIES

New travel methods will change how people get around in the future. Commuting long distances will be easier and faster than it is today. This change could have huge effects on where people live. If self-driving vehicles and flying taxis become common, cities may spread out. Some people might live longer distances from work. People may no longer need to plan where they live around access to train stations or highways. They could still get to work quickly.

New transportation methods will also change how cities look in the future. Fewer people are likely to own their own cars. If people own fewer cars, cities will need fewer parking spaces and garages. Parking areas could be put to new uses. They could be torn down and replaced with parks, gardens, or housing.

FACT
It will take about 1 billion lines of computer code to run a fully self-driving car. That's nearly 1,000 times more code than what was used to land Apollo 11 on the moon in 1969.

Self-driving cars could give people time to read, send messages, or even nap on their way to work.

TRAVEL BEYOND EARTH

There's a good chance space travel will also be part of future transportation. The Aurora Station space hotel is scheduled to open in the 2020s. It will constantly circle Earth. Plans for a moon base are in the works too. Some experts say a moon base could be in use by 2030. Others say 2040 is more likely. Travel destinations in space will probably become more common in the next 100 years. So will the transportation to get there.

Many companies are working on vehicles to take tourists into space. They come in a variety of shapes and sizes. Some look like planes. Others are more rounded or bullet-shaped. A company called SpaceX is working on a prototype of a spacecraft called Starship. A huge rocket called Super Heavy would propel this craft. Starship would be able to hold 100 passengers. If it works as planned, Starship could take tourists to the moon and beyond.

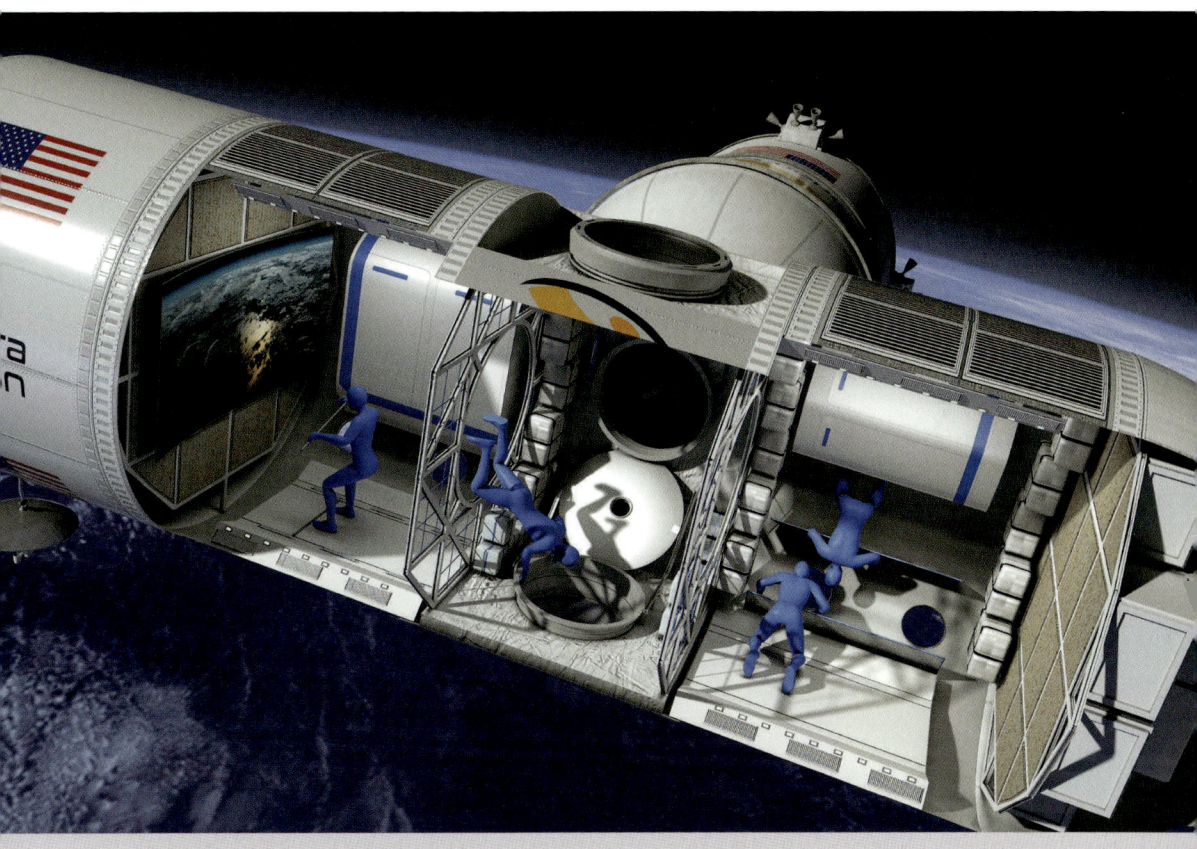

The Aurora Station space hotel can house up to four people for a maximum of 12 days.

FACT
By 2022, the Aurora Station hotel is scheduled to be in orbit. It will likely cost guests $9.5 million for a 12-day stay there, including transportation.

THE ROAD TO THE FUTURE

The exciting future of transportation involves more than just awesome vehicles. Nearly every aspect of transit could change in the coming years. That includes roads. Today most roads are made of asphalt or gravel. But people are researching all kinds of materials for use in roads. Algae, used coffee grounds, and even pig waste could be part of roads one day. Scientists are working on roads that repair themselves. These roads would contain little capsules of a chemical. When cracks start to form, this chemical would expand and fill in the cracks.

The only certainty about the future of transportation is that things are bound to change. Businesspeople may blast off by rocket for a meeting across the world. Families might take a vacation in space. Whether as a traveler or a worker, chances are you will be a part of the exciting future of transportation!

New forms of transportation could change the landscape of our cities.

Self-repairing roads could save people millions of dollars on road construction costs.

43

TIMELINE

1807: The first steamboat, the *Clemont*, makes its maiden voyage. It was invented by Robert Fulton.

1852: Jules Henri Giffard's steam-powered airship makes its first flight in France.

1879: The world's first electric train goes on display in Germany.

1886: The Benz Patent Motorwagen is patented by German inventor Karl Benz. It is widely recognized as the first modern car.

1903: Orville and Wilbur Wright have the first successful airplane flight at Kitty Hawk, North Carolina.

1928: Henry Ford's flying car, the Flivver, crashes, killing test pilot Harry J. Brooks.

1952: Thomas Moore successfully tests a rocket pack that propels him into the air, but only for a few seconds.

1959: The hovercraft, a new vehicle able to travel over both land and sea, is launched for the first time.

1976: The first commercial flight of the supersonic aircraft Concorde takes place.

1984: The first maglev system opens in Birmingham, England.

1997: The Toyota Prius is released. It is the first mass-produced hybrid car. Hybrid cars run on a combination of electricity and gas or diesel fuel.

2001: The Segway, a two-wheeled, self-balancing scooter, is available to the public.

2004: Shanghai's maglev system begins operating between Pudong International Airport and the city's outskirts.

2009: Google begins its self-driving car project, now known as Waymo.

2015-2016: The first around-the-globe flight in a solar airplane is completed.

2016: The world's first Hyperloop manufacturing plant opens in Las Vegas, Nevada.

2017: The government of the United Kingdom announces that new vehicles that run on fossil fuels would be banned from sale by 2040.

GLOSSARY

airship (AIR-ship)—a lighter-than-air aircraft with engines and a passenger compartment

app (AP)—a computer program that performs a task

autonomous (aw-TAH-nuh-muhss)—able to control oneself

biofuel (BYE-oh-fyoo-uhl)—a fuel made of, or produced from, plant material

booster (BOO-stur)—a rocket that powers a spacecraft

drag (DRAG)—a force that resists the motion of an object

drone (DROHN)—an unmanned, remote-controlled aircraft or missile

emissions (ee-MI-shuhnz)—substances released into the air

fossil fuels (FAH-suhl FYOOLZ)—fuels made from the remains of ancient organisms; coal, oil, and natural gas are fossil fuels

Global Positioning System (GLOH-buhl puh-ZI-shuh-ning SISS-tuhm)—an electronic tool used to find the location of an object; also called GPS

maglev (MAG-lev)—a train that is driven by magnetic force; stands for magnetic levitation

prototype (PROH-tuh-tipe)—the first version of an invention that tests an idea to see if it will work

supersonic (soo-pur-SON-ik)—past the speed of sound

transit (TRAN-sit)—a system for carrying people or goods from one place to another

READ MORE

Bethea, Nikole Brooks. *High-Tech Highways and Super Skyways: The Next 100 Years Of Transportation.* North Mankato, MN: Capstone Press, 2017.

Chandler, Matt. *The Tech Behind Self-Driving Cars.* North Mankato, MN: Capstone Press, 2020.

Chow-Miller, Ian. *How Self-Driving Cars Work.* New York: Cavendish Square Publishing, 2019.

INTERNET SITES

Are Driverless Cars a Good Idea?
junior.scholastic.com/issues/2017-18/112017/are-driverless-cars-a-good-idea.html

ESA Helps Students to Test Hyperloop Technology
www.esa.int/kids/en/learn/Technology/Useful_space/ESA_helps_students_to_test_hyperloop_technology

See the Future of Transportation
time.com/4189074/transportation-future/

INDEX

airplanes, 14, 24, 26, 28, 30, 36, 40
    Aurora D8, 26
    Concorde, the, 30
    electric airplanes, 28, 32
    HYTEX, 30
    pilotless airplanes, 28, 29
airships, 14
    Flying Whales, 14
    Hindenburg, 14
Aurora Station, 40, 41
autonomous ships, 12
    Yara Birkeland, 13

biofuels, 32

drones, 18

flying cars, 5, 16, 17, 18, 38
    AeroMobil, 16
    Ford Flivver, 17
    Pal-V Liberty, 16
Ford, Henry, 17
fossil fuels, 26, 28, 32, 33
futures studies, 6

Global Positioning System (GPS), 34

hydrogen, 14, 32, 36
Hyperloop, 4, 24, 25

intersection managers, 34

jet packs, 4

maglev trains, 20–22, 24
    super maglevs, 22

Pearson, Ian, 24

roads, 8, 16, 42

self-driving cars, 4, 8–10, 11, 18, 34, 38
SpaceLiner, 36, 37
space travel, 40, 42
Starship, 40

VTOL vehicles, 18